HOW CAN I MAKE A DIFFERENCE?

A guided journal

by Stacey Montgomery

Written and illustrated by Stacey Montgomery

Published in the United States by
Believe and Be Brave, Aurora, IL
believeandbebrave.com

BELIEVE AND BE BRAVE is a trademark of Stacey Montgomery.

ISBN: 979-8-218-71459-8

Printed in the United States of America

We'd love to hear from you:
Email: hello@believeandbebrave.com
Facebook: @believeandbebrave
Instagram: @believeandbebrave

"YOUR KINDNESS IS A SPARK. ONE SMALL ACTION CAN LIGHT UP SOMEONE'S WORLD—AND BRIGHTEN YOURS TOO. SO, SHINE YOUR LIGHT AND WATCH IT SPREAD."

Stacey Montgomery

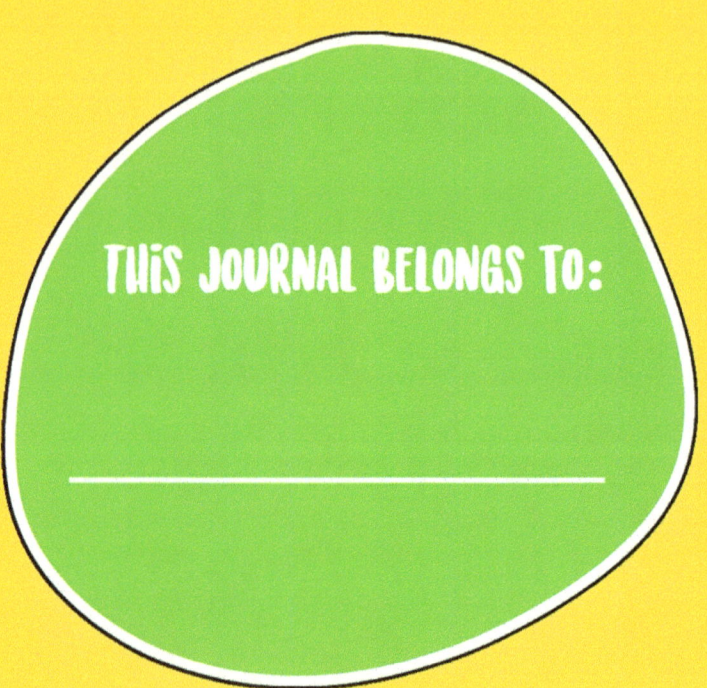

THIS JOURNAL BELONGS TO:

_____

WHY DOES MAKING A DIFFERENCE MATTER?

It might seem like your actions are too small to matter. But even the tiniest acts of kindness can create a ripple effect. You never know how a kind word, a helping hand, or a simple smile might change someone's day or even their life.

HOW HELPING OTHERS HELPS YOU TOO

✅ It's a Mood Booster. Doing something nice can make you feel happier.

✅ It Builds Confidence. When you help others, you prove to yourself that you have something to offer.

✅ It Creates Connections. Being kind helps you make friends and build a sense of community.

SIMPLE WAYS TO MAKE A DIFFERENCE

✅ Listen first. Sometimes, just being there is enough.

✅ Lend a hand. Offer to help with a chore, a project, or even just carrying something.

✅ Be kind, even when no one's watching. Your actions matter, whether big or small.

USE THIS JOURNAL TO DISCOVER HOW SMALL ACTIONS CAN LEAD TO BIG CHANGES FOR YOU AND FOR OTHERS.

TIPS FOR USING THIS GUIDED JOURNAL

In these pages, you'll answer questions, think about your strengths, dream up ways to help others, and celebrate all the good you can do. There are no wrong answers. Write what you feel, doodle in the margins, and even leave things blank if you're not sure yet. This is your space.

✔ **Pick Your Favorite Spot:** Find a cozy place where you like to write — your bed, the living room floor, or a comfy chair.

✔ **Make It a Habit:** Spend a few minutes with your journal every day. Starting with the first few pages is a great way to begin.

✔ **Write After You Help:** When you complete a volunteer project, write about it while it's still fresh in your mind.

✔ **Grab Some Color:** This guided journal is about your creativity. So, in addition to a pencil or pen, keep crayons or colored pencils nearby. You'll find chances to write, color, doodle, and draw.

✔ **Talk About Big Ideas:** Use this journal on your own or talk about it with a parent, grandparent, teacher, or another adult. You might come up with big ideas or questions about problems you don't fully understand or can't fix alone. Ask for help or talk them through.

✔ **Team Up If You Want:** This journal is about you making a difference. But it's okay to work with a friend, sibling, or a group like your scout troop or sports team.

Now get comfy and get started! You're about to learn how awesome and powerful you are and share it with the world through your kindness.

When people think about volunteering, they may use different words like serving others, helping, supporting, or giving back. While each has its own special meaning, they all share something in common– they all mean being kind and doing something good for others!

SERVING OTHERS
Doing something to help others and make their lives better. Example– Writing letters to thank veterans for their service.

VOLUNTEERING
Doing something nice without being asked or paid – just because you care. Example– Cleaning up litter in a park.

HELPING
Doing something kind to make things easier for someone else. Example– Helping to put away the groceries.

MAKING A DIFFERENCE
Using your actions and talents to help others and make their lives better. Example– Helping a younger sibling learn how to ride a bike.

GIVING BACK
Helping others or your community to make a positive impact. Example– After enjoying many great books, donating books to a library.

SUPPORTING
Being there for someone by encouraging them, listening, or providing what they need. Example– Cheering for a friend at their soccer game so they feel encouraged.

Grab your crayons or colored pencils and fill this page with even more words, phrases, and doodles about volunteering, helping others, and being kind. There are a few words and doodles to get you started. Now, add more to make it your own!

Be Kind

happy

feel good

☺

♡

better world

Think about a time when you did something kind for someone else. It may have seemed small, but it made a big difference. Maybe you smiled at someone who looked a little sad, helped a classmate pick up their supplies after they spilled, or did a chore at home without being asked.

Describe a small kindness you did for someone else. _____

_____

_____

How did doing a small kindness for someone else make you feel?

Proud   Happy   Thankful   Kind   Brave

Think of a time when someone did something kind for you. It might have seemed small to them, but it made a big difference to you. Maybe a friend invited you to play when you felt left out, or a family member helped you with something hard.

Describe a small kindness someone did for you. _____

_____

_____

How did you feel when someone did this kind thing for you?

Thankful   Loved   Happy   Confident   Surprised

SELF-DOUBT

Sometimes we start to question our ability to do things before we even try. This is called negative self-talk. It happens when we begin to doubt ourselves or think we are not good enough. You might have had some thoughts or questions like these when thinking about helping others.

What if I can't talk?

What if I wear glasses?

What if I always make mistakes?

What if it takes me a long time to do things?

What if I'm not that tall?

What if I have autism?

What if I'm afraid to speak in front of people?

What if I use a wheelchair?

What if I need help reading or writing?

These thoughts happen, but check out the next page!

EVEN IF YOU'VE HAD
ANY OF THOSE THOUGHTS,
DON'T LET THEM STOP YOU!
YOU HAVE THE POWER
TO MAKE A DIFFERENCE.
YOU ARE READY.
YOU ARE CAPABLE.
YOU ARE NEEDED.
YOU CAN HELP!

These aren't just words. They're you. Say them out loud!

I AM READY!

I AM A DIFFERENCE-MAKER!

I AM CAPABLE!

I AM NEEDED!

I AM HELPFUL!

I AM POWERFUL!

Look in the mirror. What do you see? Draw yourself in the frame, just as you are. You already have what you need to make a difference. Being yourself is more than enough.

I AM ENOUGH!

YOUR STRENGTHS

Did you know the things you love to do and are good at can help others? For example, if you love animals, you could volunteer at an animal shelter by helping to feed the animals. If you're great at reading, you could read stories to younger kids. Using your talents is a great way to make a difference!

Enjoy writing ⟶ Write kind letters to veterans.

Enjoy cooking ⟶ Bake cookies or help prepare snacks for a local shelter or first responders.

Great with pet care ⟶ Volunteer at an animal shelter and help care for animals.

Enjoy arts and crafts ⟶ Create cheerful room decor for nursing home residents or decorate meal bags for a food pantry.

Enjoy reading ⟶ Read books to younger kids at a library or community center.

Enjoy physical activity ⟶ Help clean up a park, rake leaves, or shovel snow for neighbors.

Friendly and outgoing ⟶ Be a buddy to a new student at school or welcome visitors at an event.

Great at organizing ⟶ Help sort donations at a food bank or school supply drive.

Tech-savvy ⟶ Teach a younger sibling or grandparent how to use a tablet or computer.

Love sports ⟶ Help coach younger kids.

By using your unique talents, you can make a positive impact in your community! What will you do to help?

Think about two things you really love to do or you know you do well. Then, write down how you can use each of these talents to help others or make your community better. For example, if you're good at math, you can use that talent to count donations at a food drive or figure out how many supplies are needed for a project.

Something that I'm really good at is: _____

_____

I can use this talent to help someone or make my community better by: _____

_____

Something that I'm really good at is: _____

_____

I can use this talent to help someone or make my community better by: _____

_____

You have the power to make a difference with your talents.
Keep thinking of ways to use them for good!

WAYS TO HELP

There are many places where help is needed in your neighborhood, school, town, country, and even around the world. Here are 10 important areas where you can make a difference!

Homelessness
Helping people who don't have a home by donating supplies, making care

Elderly Support
Helping older adults who may be lonely by spending time with them, listening to their stories, and helping with daily tasks.

Disability Support
Creating welcoming spaces and offering help to people with disabilities.

Environmental Care
Taking care of nature by recycling, saving energy, and cleaning up trash.

Veterans Support
Thanking veterans for their service with letters, cards, or care packages.

Animals
Caring for pets, farm animals, and wildlife by helping shelters or protecting their habitats.

Coping with Illness
Helping people who are sick by showing kindness and support.

Global Issues
Helping people around the world by supporting disaster relief or other important global causes.

Anti-Bullying
Standing up against bullying and helping to create a safe and friendly environment for everyone.

Food Insecurity
Helping people who don't have enough to eat by donating food or volunteering at food pantries.

Design a t-shirt you'd wear when you volunteer. Include words or a message that show you're ready to help. Think about what kindness and service mean to you as you create your design.

GOAL-SETTING & PLANNING

Not everyone prefers to help in the same way. Answer these 6 questions to discover how you do your best work when helping others.

1. When someone needs help, what do you do first?
   A. Jump in and help right away.
   B. Think of a plan to fix the problem.
   C. Say something kind to cheer them up.
   D. Ask friends to help too.

2. Which activity sounds the most fun?
   A. Feeding animals or cleaning up a park.
   B. Starting a fundraiser for a cause.
   C. Writing kind notes to people.
   D. Working together with friends to help.

3. A friend is sad. What do you do?
   A. Give them a hug or sit with them.
   B. Think of a way to solve their problem.
   C. Tell them something nice about themselves.
   D. Plan a fun activity with friends to cheer them up.

4. What kind of stories do you like the most?
   A. Stories about people helping others.
   B. Stories about kids solving big problems.
   C. Stories where characters are kind to each other.
   D. Stories about teams working together.

5. If you could create a project to help others, what would it be?
   A. Making care packages or cleaning up a park.
   B. A big fundraiser to help people in need.
   C. Writing letters or making cards for others.
   D. Planning a group project with friends.

6. How do you think you would like volunteering?
   A. Mostly by myself.
   B. With my family.
   C. With my friends.
   D. It doesn't matter. I just want to help!

MY HELPER STYLE

Here are your results! There are many ways to help others, and most of us help in different ways. However, based on your answers, you might find that you enjoy helping in a certain way the most!

The Hands-On Helper (Mostly A's)

You like to jump in and help right away! You do your best work when you're doing something active, like making care packages, helping animals, or cleaning up a park.

The Big Thinker (Mostly B's)

You love coming up with big ideas! You're great at making plans and solving problems. You might enjoy starting a fundraiser, organizing donations, or raising awareness for an important cause.

The Encourager (Mostly C's)

You make people feel special! You love using words and small acts of kindness to brighten someone's day. You might enjoy writing kind letters, making posters, or helping classmates feel included.

The Team Leader (Mostly D's)

You believe that teamwork makes everything better! You like organizing group projects and helping everyone work together. You might enjoy leading a service club, planning events, or getting friends to help with a cause.

What do YOU think? Which type of helper are you?

◯ Hands-On Helper ◯ Big Thinker ◯ Encourager ◯ Team Leader

What makes you say that? _____

_____

_____

Are you excited to get started volunteering, but are not sure where to begin? Start by thinking about the needs in your own community, where you've volunteered before, and organizations that regularly offer opportunities to volunteer.

Who in your community might need your help?

Think about people like someone without a home, someone who needs help getting food, first responders, sick kids, or older neighbors. Write down 2 specific groups or people in your community who need help.

1. _____

2. _____

Where have you volunteered in the past?

Where have you volunteered before? Think about the different places where you've helped out, such as with family, a group like the scouts, school, or your church. Write down 2 places you've volunteered.

1. _____

2. _____

What organizations in your community could use extra help?

Think about local food pantries, animal rescues, libraries, community centers, or any other organizations that help people in need. Write down 2 specific organizations in your community where you could offer help.

1. _____

2. _____

BRAINSTORMING IDEAS

Think about the type of helper you are, the causes that matter most to you, and the people in your community who need help. Also, consider local organizations that offer opportunities to volunteer. Write 7 ideas for how you want to help others. These could be names of organizations, problems you want to help fix, new service project ideas, or ways you can make a difference.

Idea #1 _____
_____
_____
_____

Idea #2 _____
_____
_____
_____

Idea #3 _____
_____
_____
_____

Idea #4

_____
_____
_____
_____

Idea #5

_____
_____
_____
_____

Idea #6

_____
_____
_____
_____

Idea #7

_____
_____
_____
_____

VOLUNTEER GOAL

Setting a goal for how often you want to volunteer is a great way to stay on track and make sure you're making a difference. By setting a target, you're telling yourself that you're committed to helping others! Here are some things to think about when setting your goal:

✓ **Big or small commitment:** Your goal can be as big or small as you like. You might want to volunteer 12 times a year, 6 times a year, or 4 times a year. The important thing is to choose what works best for you!

✓ **Track your progress:** Use this journal to keep a record of how many times you volunteer. Watching your progress will keep you excited and on track to reach your goal!

✓ **Get support:** Talk to family, friends, or school groups about your goal. They can encourage you and even volunteer with you! Having a volunteer buddy can make it even more fun.

✓ **Be flexible:** Life gets busy, and that's okay! If you have to change your plan, just do what you can when you're able. The most important thing is to keep trying!

✓ **Have fun:** Volunteering is not only a great way to help, it can also be fun and rewarding! Even small acts of kindness make a big difference.

✓ **Celebrate your success:** Every time you reach a new step in this volunteering journey, be proud of what you've done! You're making a difference, and that's something to celebrate!

24

MY VOLUNTEER GOAL

Starting on _____ ,
within the next 12 months (1 year),
I, _____ ,
set a goal to volunteer ___ times to help others.

It doesn't matter if my goal is big or small.
I will do my best!

If I don't meet my goal, that's okay.
The most important thing is that I work hard
to make a difference.

Signed: _____

LEMONADE FOR A CAUSE

Nine-year-old Zoe loved riding her bike through her neighborhood. She knew every street and waved at almost everyone.

One afternoon, while biking home from the library, she noticed something strange. A group had gathered outside the Community Center. The building looked the same: gray brick walls, a faded blue door. But now a sign hung on that door: "Closed Until Further Notice."

Zoe pulled over. The Center was where she and her friends went for art classes and summer camps. Families picked up food from the pantry. Why was it closed?

She saw Ms. Rosa speaking to a few parents and overheard: "...funding cuts..."

"...hoping we can raise enough..."

Zoe's stomach dropped. Without the Center, where would kids go after school? What about the food pantry?

That night at dinner, Zoe shared what she'd seen.

"I wish there was somethin' I could do," she mumbled, poking at her mashed potatoes.

Her dad nodded. "You don't have to do somethin' huge. Little stuff counts."

Her mom smiled. "Why not come up with your own way to help?"

Zoe thought for a minute. No job. Not much money. But then – boom. A lemonade stand!

27

Zoe grabbed a notebook and started planning. She'd set up a stand by the sidewalk and make a sign saying all the money would go to the Community Center.

The next morning, her dad took her to the store for lemons, sugar, ice, and cups. Her mom helped her test the recipe. Her little brother Amari painted a big sign:

"Lemonade for the Community Center: Every Cup Counts!"

By noon, she was ready. The sun was high, and Zoe's lemonade stand was open for business. She stood behind her table with a big smile, ready to greet her first customers.

But no one showed up. Zoe started to feel nervous and began to doubt herself. "What if no one comes? What if nobody even wants lemonade?" she wondered out loud.

She reminded herself of what her dad said: Little stuff counts.

She took a deep breath. "C'mon, I worked hard on this," she told herself. "Somebody'll come by. I just gotta wait."

Finally, just as she was starting to feel discouraged, Mr. Thompson came by first.

"Look at you, Zoe! This is such a smart idea," he said, handing her a five. "Give me two cups, and keep the change."

Zoe smiled with excitement. Mrs. Patel stepped up next. "Here's a ten. Don't worry about change. The Center needs it more than I do."

Word spread quickly. Neighbors stopped by, eager to support Zoe's cause. Some people gave money without even taking lemonade.

Zoe was thrilled but also exhausted. She had to keep refilling the pitcher, squeezing lemons, stirring sugar, and greeting people all at once. Amari helped by handing out cups, and her mom kept an eye on the cash jar.

By the end of the day, Zoe and her family counted the money. She had raised $146.75! That evening, Zoe and her parents took the money to the Community Center. Ms. Rosa was still there, talking with some volunteers.

When Zoe handed her the jar, Ms. Rosa's eyes went wide. "Wait! Zoe, you did all this?"

Zoe nodded, chin high. "Yup. I had a lemonade stand. Just wanted to help out."

Ms. Rosa wiped her eyes, smiling. "Girl, this is somethin' else. Every single dollar gets us closer. But even more than that, it shows how much folks around here care."

In the days that followed, more people stepped up. Inspired by Zoe's effort, neighbors held bake sales, donated supplies, and even local businesses chipped in. Within a few weeks, the Community Center reopened for limited hours, and the food pantry was able to start helping families again.

One afternoon, as Zoe rode past the Community Center, she saw kids hanging out in front again. She knew that inside families were picking up groceries, and Ms. Rosa and volunteers were back to work.

She had only hoped to raise a little bit of money, but she had ended up inspiring the whole neighborhood. As she pedaled past her house, she glanced at her lemonade stand stored near their garage. She grinned.

"Might not be the last time I use you," she whispered. "Wonder what else I can do."

BE LIKE ZOE

Have you ever seen a problem at school, in your neighborhood, or somewhere else and really wanted to help, just like Zoe? Write about where you were, what you saw, and how it made you feel. Then, draw a picture of what you could do to help.

_____

_____

_____

_____

When you do something kind, it can inspire others to do something kind too. This is called the Ripple Effect because, just like a stone dropped in a pond creates ripples that spread out, your kindness can lead to even more kindness. In Lemonade for a Cause, Zoe's decision to raise money for the community center encouraged others to come up with their own ways to help.

Think about how your act of kindness, like volunteering, can inspire others to be kind too. Write your act of kindness in the heart. Then, in each of the rings around the heart, write what your actions might lead others to do.

HOW AMAZING IT IS
TO KNOW THAT YOUR
ABILITIES, CREATIVITY,
AND ACTIONS
-YOUR AWESOMENESS-
CAN HELP OTHERS
AND MAKE A
BIG DIFFERENCE!

Helping Starts Young

Meet James and Tess, two siblings who know a lot about helping others. Their mom started The 3:11 Project, an organization that helps people in the community who need housing, food, or clothing. Even though they have volunteered a lot with The 3:11 Project, they have a huge interest in helping others wherever they can and have volunteered in many other places. In this interview, James, 11, and Tess, 8, share their thoughts on volunteering, what they love about it, and how even small actions can make a big difference.

HOW OLD WERE YOU WHEN YOU FIRST STARTED HELPING OTHERS IN YOUR COMMUNITY?

James: 2 years old.
Tess: When I was born.

REAL KIDS IN ACTION

WHO OR WHAT INSPIRES YOU TO HELP OTHERS?

James: My mother and her persistence to keep going.

Tess: My mother and her helpfulness.

WHAT'S ONE PROJECT OR ACTIVITY YOU'VE DONE THAT MADE YOU FEEL REALLY PROUD?

James: I liked voting at school for donating to different nonprofits that help others in need.

Tess: Helping with the Lemon-aid stand for The 3:11 Project.

HOW DID YOU FEEL AFTER DOING THAT PROJECT?

James: I felt hopeful that people I helped would do better. Every grain of sand helps build a beach. So every little goal that someone achieves helps them make something better of themselves.

Tess: I felt like I did something good. I was proud. All the kids that needed help would get something they need.

DO YOU ENJOY VOLUNTEERING WITH YOUR SIBLING? WHAT'S FUN ABOUT IT?

James: I enjoy volunteering with my sibling, but she does not enjoy volunteering with me.

Tess: Yes. Because it's fun!

WHAT ADVICE WOULD YOU GIVE TO ANOTHER KID WHO WANTS TO MAKE A DIFFERENCE BUT ISN'T SURE HOW TO START?

James: Stay committed. Study others. And an idea will find you somehow.
Tess: I would tell the kids to just try to be nice and offer help.

James and Tess have helped with several different groups, but they spend most of their time volunteering with The 3:11 Project. They help collect food, clothing, and other items for people who need them. Over the years, they've worked hard with lots of other volunteers to make a difference. A newspaper even wrote about it! Here's what it said:

DAILY HELPER

THE 3:11 PROJECT GIVES HOLIDAY CHEER TO HUNDREDS OF KIDS AND SENIORS

James and Tess remind us that no matter your age, you can help make the world a better place.

EVERY LITTLE BIT HELPS

Eleven-year-old James said, "Every grain of sand helps build a beach." This means that even small acts of kindness can add up to something big. On this page, fill the beach with words that show different ways people can help, show kindness, or volunteer. You can write things you've done, things you want to do, or things you've seen others do. When everyone helps, it can make a huge difference!

MY VOLUNTEERING LOG & REFLECTION

This part of your journal is your Volunteering Log. It includes 18 sets of 2 pages to keep track of your volunteer projects. These pages give you space to record what you did, how it felt, and what you learned along the way.

Throughout this journal, you've already thought about so many important things such as what kinds of help are needed in your community, what causes you care about, how you like to help, and how your talents and interests can make a difference. These reflections have prepared you to take action – one project at a time.

On the next page, you'll find some quick and simple ideas to help you choose your next service project. Remember, even a small act of kindness can have a big impact and add sunshine to someone's day.

Why write it all down? Because reflection helps you grow.

 You'll start to notice patterns in what matters to you.

 You'll learn from your experiences – both the fun parts and the hard parts.

 You'll feel proud of your efforts and see just how much you're capable of.

And one day, you might look back on this journal and remember all the ways you made the world a little better.

This is your journey. Use these pages to tell your story.

GET STARTED HELPING

As you seek ways to help and volunteer, think about what you wrote in the pages of this journal. In addition, here are some simple ways you can volunteer and make a difference. Which one will you try first?

Lemonade Stand   Food Drive   Caring for Animals

Raise Money   Clean Up Litter   Make Greeting Cards

Clothes Drive   Toy Donation   Bake Sale

Make Hot Meals   School Supply Drive   Planting Garden

If you need help thinking of projects or understanding a problem in your community, ask a parent, grandparent, teacher, or coach — someone you trust. Let's call these people your team members. Team members are the people who help you, support you, and cheer you on. Just like you can make a difference in the community by using your power, they can help you make that difference too. Who are your team members? Use your crayons and colored pencils to make these superheroes look like you and two of your team members. Write what your superpowers are in the bubbles.

MY SERVICE JOURNEY

Date of project (when I helped): _____

Name of organization or project (where I helped): _____

_____

What problem was I helping with?

☐ Homelessness   ☐ Food Insecurity   ☐ Elderly Support

☐ Animals   ☐ Coping with Illness   ☐ Disability Support

☐ Environmental Care   ☐ Veterans Support   ☐ Other-write it here:

☐ Global Issues   ☐ Anti-Bullying   _____

What did I do to help? _____

_____

_____

How did it make me feel? Circle the feelings that describe how you felt.

🙂 Happy- I felt good about helping

😊 Proud- I was proud of my actions

🙂 Confident- I felt sure that I made a difference

🙁 Nervous- I felt unsure about what I had to do

😣 Sad- I felt sad after helping

🙂 Grateful- I felt thankful for what I have

What challenges did I face during this project? _____

_____

_____

_____

Three things that I learned:

1. _____

2. _____

3. _____

NOTES & DOODLES

Use this space to write notes about your experience, draw a picture,
or express any feelings you had while helping others.

MY SERVICE JOURNEY

Date of project (when I helped): _____

Name of organization or project (where I helped): _____

_____

What problem was I helping with?

☐ Homelessness   ☐ Food Insecurity   ☐ Elderly Support

☐ Animals   ☐ Coping with Illness ☐ Disability Support

☐ Environmental Care ☐ Veterans Support   ☐ Other—write it
                                             here:
☐ Global Issues   ☐ Anti-Bullying
                                          _____

What did I do to help? _____

_____

_____

How did it make me feel? Circle the feelings that describe how you felt.

🙂 Happy— I felt good about helping

😌 Proud— I was proud of my actions

🙂 Confident— I felt sure that I made a difference

🙁 Nervous— I felt unsure about what I had to do

😖 Sad— I felt sad after helping

🙂 Grateful— I felt thankful for what I have

What challenges did I face during this project? _____

_____

_____

_____

Three things that I learned:

1. _____

2. _____

3. _____

NOTES & DOODLES

Use this space to write notes about your experience, draw a picture,
or express any feelings you had while helping others.

MY SERVICE JOURNEY

Date of project (when I helped): _____

Name of organization or project (where I helped): _____

_____

What problem was I helping with?

☐ Homelessness ☐ Food Insecurity ☐ Elderly Support

☐ Animals ☐ Coping with Illness ☐ Disability Support

☐ Environmental Care ☐ Veterans Support ☐ Other-write it here:

☐ Global Issues ☐ Anti-Bullying _____

What did I do to help? _____

_____

_____

How did it make me feel? Circle the feelings that describe how you felt.

🙂 Happy- I felt good about helping

😌 Proud- I was proud of my actions

🙂 Confident- I felt sure that I made a difference

🙁 Nervous- I felt unsure about what I had to do

☹️ Sad- I felt sad after helping

🙂 Grateful- I felt thankful for what I have

What challenges did I face during this project? _____

_____

_____

_____

Three things that I learned:

1. _____

2. _____

3. _____

NOTES & DOODLES

Use this space to write notes about your experience, draw a picture,
or express any feelings you had while helping others.

MY SERVICE JOURNEY

Date of project (when I helped): _____

Name of organization or project (where I helped): _____

_____

What problem was I helping with?

☐ Homelessness   ☐ Food Insecurity   ☐ Elderly Support

☐ Animals   ☐ Coping with Illness   ☐ Disability Support

☐ Environmental Care   ☐ Veterans Support   ☐ Other-write it here:

☐ Global Issues   ☐ Anti-Bullying   _____

What did I do to help? _____

_____

_____

How did it make me feel? Circle the feelings that describe how you felt.

🙂 Happy- I felt good about helping

😌 Proud- I was proud of my actions

🙂 Confident- I felt sure that I made a difference

😕 Nervous- I felt unsure about what I had to do

☹️ Sad- I felt sad after helping

🙂 Grateful- I felt thankful for what I have

What challenges did I face during this project? _____

_____

_____

_____

Three things that I learned:

1. _____
2. _____
3. _____

NOTES & DOODLES

Use this space to write notes about your experience, draw a picture,
or express any feelings you had while helping others.

MY SERVICE JOURNEY

Date of project (when I helped): _____

Name of organization or project (where I helped): _____

_____

What problem was I helping with?

☐ Homelessness   ☐ Food Insecurity   ☐ Elderly Support

☐ Animals   ☐ Coping with Illness   ☐ Disability Support

☐ Environmental Care   ☐ Veterans Support   ☐ Other-write it here:

☐ Global Issues   ☐ Anti-Bullying   _____

What did I do to help? _____

_____

_____

How did it make me feel? Circle the feelings that describe how you felt.

🙂 Happy- I felt good about helping   😟 Nervous- I felt unsure about what I had to do

😊 Proud- I was proud of my actions   🙁 Sad- I felt sad after helping

😃 Confident- I felt sure that I made a difference   🙂 Grateful- I felt thankful for what I have

What challenges did I face during this project? _____

_____

_____

_____

Three things that I learned:

1. _____

2. _____

3. _____

NOTES & DOODLES

Use this space to write notes about your experience, draw a picture,
or express any feelings you had while helping others.

MY SERVICE JOURNEY

Date of project (when I helped): _____

Name of organization or project (where I helped): _____

_____

What problem was I helping with?

☐ Homelessness   ☐ Food Insecurity   ☐ Elderly Support

☐ Animals   ☐ Coping with Illness   ☐ Disability Support

☐ Environmental Care   ☐ Veterans Support   ☐ Other–write it here:

☐ Global Issues   ☐ Anti-Bullying   _____

What did I do to help? _____

_____

_____

How did it make me feel? Circle the feelings that describe how you felt.

🙂 Happy– I felt good about helping   🙁 Nervous– I felt unsure about what I had to do

😌 Proud– I was proud of my actions   😣 Sad– I felt sad after helping

🙂 Confident– I felt sure that I made a difference   🙂 Grateful– I felt thankful for what I have

MY SERVICE JOURNEY

What challenges did I face during this project? _____

_____

_____

_____

Three things that I learned:

1. _____

2. _____

3. _____

NOTES & DOODLES

Use this space to write notes about your experience, draw a picture,
or express any feelings you had while helping others.

MY SERVICE JOURNEY

Date of project (when I helped): _____

Name of organization or project (where I helped): _____

_____

What problem was I helping with?

☐ Homelessness   ☐ Food Insecurity   ☐ Elderly Support

☐ Animals   ☐ Coping with Illness   ☐ Disability Support

☐ Environmental Care   ☐ Veterans Support   ☐ Other-write it here:

☐ Global Issues   ☐ Anti-Bullying   _____

What did I do to help? _____

_____

_____

How did it make me feel? Circle the feelings that describe how you felt.

🙂 Happy— I felt good about helping

😊 Proud— I was proud of my actions

🙂 Confident— I felt sure that I made a difference

🙁 Nervous— I felt unsure about what I had to do

😣 Sad— I felt sad after helping

🙂 Grateful— I felt thankful for what I have

MY SERVICE JOURNEY

What challenges did I face during this project? _____

_____

_____

_____

Three things that I learned:

1. _____

2. _____

3. _____

NOTES & DOODLES

Use this space to write notes about your experience, draw a picture,
or express any feelings you had while helping others.

MY SERVICE JOURNEY

Date of project (when I helped):_____

Name of organization or project (where I helped): _____

_____

What problem was I helping with?

☐ Homelessness   ☐ Food Insecurity   ☐ Elderly Support

☐ Animals   ☐ Coping with Illness   ☐ Disability Support

☐ Environmental Care   ☐ Veterans Support   ☐ Other-write it here:

☐ Global Issues   ☐ Anti-Bullying   _____

What did I do to help? _____

_____

_____

How did it make me feel? Circle the feelings that describe how you felt.

😃 Happy- I felt good about helping   😟 Nervous- I felt unsure about what I had to do

😊 Proud- I was proud of my actions   😣 Sad- I felt sad after helping

😃 Confident- I felt sure that I made a difference   🙂 Grateful- I felt thankful for what I have

56

MY SERVICE JOURNEY

What challenges did I face during this project? _____

_____

_____

_____

Three things that I learned:

1. _____

2. _____

3. _____

NOTES & DOODLES

Use this space to write notes about your experience, draw a picture,
or express any feelings you had while helping others.

MY SERVICE JOURNEY

Date of project (when I helped): _____

Name of organization or project (where I helped): _____

_____

What problem was I helping with?

☐ Homelessness   ☐ Food Insecurity   ☐ Elderly Support

☐ Animals   ☐ Coping with Illness   ☐ Disability Support

☐ Environmental Care   ☐ Veterans Support   ☐ Other-write it here:

☐ Global Issues   ☐ Anti-Bullying   _____

What did I do to help? _____

_____

_____

How did it make me feel? Circle the feelings that describe how you felt.

🙂 Happy- I felt good about helping   🙁 Nervous- I felt unsure about what I had to do

😊 Proud- I was proud of my actions   😞 Sad- I felt sad after helping

🙂 Confident- I felt sure that I made a difference   🙂 Grateful- I felt thankful for what I have

58

What challenges did I face during this project? _____

_____

_____

_____

Three things that I learned:

1. _____

2. _____

3. _____

NOTES & DOODLES

Use this space to write notes about your experience, draw a picture,
or express any feelings you had while helping others.

MY SERVICE JOURNEY

Date of project (when I helped): _____

Name of organization or project (where I helped): _____

_____

What problem was I helping with?

☐ Homelessness ☐ Food Insecurity ☐ Elderly Support

☐ Animals ☐ Coping with Illness ☐ Disability Support

☐ Environmental Care ☐ Veterans Support ☐ Other-write it here:

☐ Global Issues ☐ Anti-Bullying _____

What did I do to help? _____

_____

_____

How did it make me feel? Circle the feelings that describe how you felt.

🙂 Happy- I felt good about helping

😊 Proud- I was proud of my actions

🙂 Confident- I felt sure that I made a difference

😕 Nervous- I felt unsure about what I had to do

☹️ Sad- I felt sad after helping

🙂 Grateful- I felt thankful for what I have

What challenges did I face during this project? _____

_____

_____

_____

Three things that I learned:

1. _____

2. _____

3. _____

NOTES & DOODLES

Use this space to write notes about your experience, draw a picture,
or express any feelings you had while helping others.

MY SERVICE JOURNEY

Date of project (when I helped): _____

Name of organization or project (where I helped): _____

_____

What problem was I helping with?

☐ Homelessness   ☐ Food Insecurity   ☐ Elderly Support

☐ Animals   ☐ Coping with Illness   ☐ Disability Support

☐ Environmental Care ☐ Veterans Support   ☐ Other—write it here:

☐ Global Issues   ☐ Anti-Bullying   _____

What did I do to help? _____

_____

_____

How did it make me feel? Circle the feelings that describe how you felt.

🙂 Happy— I felt good about helping   😕 Nervous— I felt unsure about what I had to do

😊 Proud— I was proud of my actions   ☹️ Sad— I felt sad after helping

😃 Confident— I felt sure that I made a difference   🙂 Grateful— I felt thankful for what I have

What challenges did I face during this project? _____

_____

_____

_____

Three things that I learned:

1. _____

2. _____

3. _____

NOTES & DOODLES

Use this space to write notes about your experience, draw a picture,
or express any feelings you had while helping others.

MY SERVICE JOURNEY

Date of project (when I helped): _____

Name of organization or project (where I helped): _____

_____

What problem was I helping with?

☐ Homelessness   ☐ Food Insecurity   ☐ Elderly Support

☐ Animals   ☐ Coping with Illness   ☐ Disability Support

☐ Environmental Care   ☐ Veterans Support   ☐ Other—write it here:

☐ Global Issues   ☐ Anti-Bullying   _____

What did I do to help? _____

_____

_____

How did it make me feel? Circle the feelings that describe how you felt.

🙂 Happy– I felt good about helping

😊 Proud– I was proud of my actions

🙂 Confident– I felt sure that I made a difference

🙁 Nervous– I felt unsure about what I had to do

☹️ Sad– I felt sad after helping

🙂 Grateful– I felt thankful for what I have

64

What challenges did I face during this project? _____

_____

_____

_____

Three things that I learned:

1. _____

2. _____

3. _____

NOTES & DOODLES

Use this space to write notes about your experience, draw a picture,
or express any feelings you had while helping others.

MY SERVICE JOURNEY

Date of project (when I helped): _____

Name of organization or project (where I helped): _____

_____

What problem was I helping with?

- ☐ Homelessness
- ☐ Food Insecurity
- ☐ Elderly Support
- ☐ Animals
- ☐ Coping with Illness
- ☐ Disability Support
- ☐ Environmental Care
- ☐ Veterans Support
- ☐ Other-write it here:
- ☐ Global Issues
- ☐ Anti-Bullying

_____

What did I do to help? _____

_____

_____

How did it make me feel? Circle the feelings that describe how you felt.

- 🙂 Happy- I felt good about helping
- 😕 Nervous- I felt unsure about what I had to do
- 😌 Proud- I was proud of my actions
- 🙁 Sad- I felt sad after helping
- 😃 Confident- I felt sure that I made a difference
- 🙂 Grateful- I felt thankful for what I have

MY SERVICE JOURNEY

What challenges did I face during this project? _____

_____

_____

_____

Three things that I learned:

1. _____

2. _____

3. _____

NOTES & DOODLES

Use this space to write notes about your experience, draw a picture,
or express any feelings you had while helping others.

MY SERVICE JOURNEY

Date of project (when I helped): _____

Name of organization or project (where I helped): _____

_____

What problem was I helping with?

☐ Homelessness   ☐ Food Insecurity   ☐ Elderly Support

☐ Animals   ☐ Coping with Illness   ☐ Disability Support

☐ Environmental Care   ☐ Veterans Support   ☐ Other—write it here:

☐ Global Issues   ☐ Anti-Bullying   _____

What did I do to help? _____

_____

_____

How did it make me feel? Circle the feelings that describe how you felt.

🙂 Happy— I felt good about helping

😊 Proud— I was proud of my actions

🙂 Confident— I felt sure that I made a difference

🙁 Nervous— I felt unsure about what I had to do

😣 Sad— I felt sad after helping

🙂 Grateful— I felt thankful for what I have

What challenges did I face during this project? _____

_____

_____

_____

Three things that I learned:

1. _____

2. _____

3. _____

NOTES & DOODLES

Use this space to write notes about your experience, draw a picture,
or express any feelings you had while helping others.

MY SERVICE JOURNEY

Date of project (when I helped): _____

Name of organization or project (where I helped): _____

_____

What problem was I helping with?

☐ Homelessness   ☐ Food Insecurity   ☐ Elderly Support

☐ Animals   ☐ Coping with Illness   ☐ Disability Support

☐ Environmental Care   ☐ Veterans Support   ☐ Other-write it here:

☐ Global Issues   ☐ Anti-Bullying   _____

What did I do to help? _____

_____

_____

How did it make me feel? Circle the feelings that describe how you felt.

🙂 Happy- I felt good about helping   🙁 Nervous- I felt unsure about what I had to do

😌 Proud- I was proud of my actions   😣 Sad- I felt sad after helping

🙂 Confident- I felt sure that I made a difference   🙂 Grateful- I felt thankful for what I have

70

MY SERVICE JOURNEY

What challenges did I face during this project? _____

_____

_____

_____

Three things that I learned:

1. _____

2. _____

3. _____

NOTES & DOODLES

Use this space to write notes about your experience, draw a picture,
or express any feelings you had while helping others.

MY SERViCE JOURNEY

Date of project (when I helped): _____

Name of organization or project (where I helped): _____

_____

What problem was I helping with?

☐ Homelessness   ☐ Food Insecurity   ☐ Elderly Support

☐ Animals   ☐ Coping with Illness ☐ Disability Support

☐ Environmental Care ☐ Veterans Support   ☐ Other-write it
                                             here:

☐ Global Issues   ☐ Anti-Bullying   _____

What did I do to help? _____

_____

_____

How did it make me feel? Circle the feelings that describe how you felt.

🙂 Happy- I felt good about helping   🙁 Nervous- I felt unsure
                                                about what I had to do

😌 Proud- I was proud of my actions   😣 Sad- I felt sad after helping

🙂 Confident- I felt sure that I   🙂 Grateful- I felt thankful for
   made a difference   what I have

What challenges did I face during this project? _____

_____

_____

_____

Three things that I learned:

1. _____

2. _____

3. _____

NOTES & DOODLES

Use this space to write notes about your experience, draw a picture,
or express any feelings you had while helping others.

MY SERVICE JOURNEY

Date of project (when I helped): _____

Name of organization or project (where I helped): _____

_____

What problem was I helping with?

☐ Homelessness   ☐ Food Insecurity   ☐ Elderly Support

☐ Animals   ☐ Coping with Illness   ☐ Disability Support

☐ Environmental Care   ☐ Veterans Support   ☐ Other-write it here:

☐ Global Issues   ☐ Anti-Bullying   _____

What did I do to help? _____

_____

_____

How did it make me feel? Circle the feelings that describe how you felt.

🙂 Happy- I felt good about helping

😌 Proud- I was proud of my actions

🙂 Confident- I felt sure that I made a difference

🙁 Nervous- I felt unsure about what I had to do

☹️ Sad- I felt sad after helping

🙂 Grateful- I felt thankful for what I have

What challenges did I face during this project? _____

_____

_____

_____

Three things that I learned:

1. _____

2. _____

3. _____

NOTES & DOODLES

Use this space to write notes about your experience, draw a picture,
or express any feelings you had while helping others.

MY SERVICE JOURNEY

Date of project (when I helped): _____

Name of organization or project (where I helped): _____

_____

What problem was I helping with?

- ☐ Homelessness
- ☐ Food Insecurity
- ☐ Elderly Support
- ☐ Animals
- ☐ Coping with Illness
- ☐ Disability Support
- ☐ Environmental Care
- ☐ Veterans Support
- ☐ Other-write it here:
- ☐ Global Issues
- ☐ Anti-Bullying

_____

What did I do to help? _____

_____

_____

How did it make me feel? Circle the feelings that describe how you felt.

- 😃 Happy- I felt good about helping
- 🙁 Nervous- I felt unsure about what I had to do
- 😌 Proud- I was proud of my actions
- 😣 Sad- I felt sad after helping
- 🙂 Confident- I felt sure that I made a difference
- 🙂 Grateful- I felt thankful for what I have

76

What challenges did I face during this project? _____

_____

_____

_____

Three things that I learned:

1. _____

2. _____

3. _____

NOTES & DOODLES

Use this space to write notes about your experience, draw a picture,
or express any feelings you had while helping others.

REFLECTION

Look at everything you've done! You took action and showed how much one person can make a difference.

- ⭐ You found ways to help.
- ⭐ You showed kindness, courage, and determination.
- ⭐ You used your superpowers – your strengths and the things that make you who you are to make a difference.
- ⭐ You worked hard, helped others, and showed the power of believing in yourself.

Take a moment to celebrate yourself! Repeat the following out loud:

"I am proud of who I am and what I can do."

Now create 4 of your own "I am" statements!

I AM _____

I AM _____

I AM _____

I AM _____

Use this space to chart your volunteering journey. Look back at the projects in your My Service Log. Each one is like a building block — every act of service adds to your impact.

Draw one block for as many as can fit. Use different size blocks based on the size of the project. Label each block with the project name or a memory from the experience.

Start with the sample blocks at the bottom, then add more blocks to build your own structure. Add color with crayons or colored pencils!

[This page is to be completed by an adult.]

You Made a Difference!

CERTIFICATE OF RECOGNITION

This certificate is proudly presented to

_____

In recognition of volunteering and making a difference by:

_____

_____

CONGRATULATIONS!

You're amazing and powerful. Keep believing in yourself.
Remember that your kindness and actions made a difference!

Presented by: _____ Date: _____

www.ingramcontent.com/pod-product-compliance
Lightning Source LLC
Chambersburg PA
CBHW041630140626
46547CB00031B/1951